Opening a Red Bull Bar&Store in Milan

Mauro Tommaso De Candia

& his staff

TABLE OF CONTENTS

1. Introduction
2. SWOT Analysis & Project Charter
   SWOT Analysis
   Project Charter
3. WBS & Milestones
   WBS
   Milestones
4. Description of task activities
5. OBS & RAEW Matrix
6. Logical net and GANTT
   The Logical Network
   The Gantt Chart
7. CBS & Cost analysis
8. Appendix:

1. INTRODUCTION

The Red Bull company is an Austrian company selling the Red Bull energy drink. It exists on the market for 25 years and employs 8,966 people in 165 countries all over the world. Red Bull is the most popular energy drink in the world selling 5,2 billion cans in 2012.

Red Bull is marketed through strong advertising campaigns, sport events, sport team ownerships, celebrity endorsements and music, owning their own record label.

Now Red Bull wants to open a Red Bull Bar&Store as a new way of promoting its brand. The first bar will be open in Milan, but the company plans further expansion, if this project will be a success. The main aim of this project is to strengthen the brand's image, gain new customers and enter new markets. Red Bull wants to show its product in different way by selling Red Bull drink mixed with other beverages.

Our task, as a managing team, is to plan the whole project. We need to organize the work, find appropriate resources, set the deadlines and prepare costs analysis, in order to achieve our goal which is the opening of the Red Bull Bar&Store in Milan.

To do that we will use specific tools, such as WBS, OBS, RAEW Matrix, Logical Network, the Gantt chart, CBS and cost analysis.

In the WBS (Work Breakdown Structure) we decompose the project into smaller components such as phases and different level activities. Thanks to the WBS chart, it is clear what has to be done and what are the milestones of the project (specific results that should be achieved during the project realization).

The aim of the OBS (Organizational Breakdown Structure) is to decide, who is responsible for which task. The OBS chart is the presentation of all the people involved in realizing the project.

On the basis of WBS and OBS, we prepare the RAEW matrix (Responsibility Authority Expertise Work), which is the composition of both activities and people responsible for their realization. After preparing the RAEW matrix we have the clear view over every phase of the project, we know who has the responsibility for all the actions and decisions, who controls and judges the actions of other, who expertise the work and finally who are the workers that are responsible for physical and mental effort directed at doing each parts of the project.

After preparing the RAEW matrix, we have to focus on time planning. We need to decide what the duration of every task is, when the activities start and finish, what are the relations between all the tasks. Basically, we establish the calendar of our project. To do that, we prepare the Logical Network and the Gantt chart. The Logical Network is a visual representation of the sequence of all the activities in the project, it shows which activity proceed and follows another one. The Gantt chart represents the evolution of the project, including the relations between the tasks, their durations and also work in progress.

The last thing we do is CBS (Cost Breakdown Structure) which helps us to answer the question how much the whole project cost. CBS is a chart which is the development of WBS and indicates where all the costs are allocated.

2. SWOT ANALYSIS & PROJECT CHARTER

SWOT Analysis

The first step in planning our project was to issue a SWOT – Analysis in order to evaluate the Strengths, Weaknesses, Opportunities and Threats which are involved in our Red Bull Bar&Store Opening project and to identify the internal and external factors that are favorable and unfavorable to achieving the objective.

SWOT ANALYSIS

Group Nr.:

PROJECT TITLE: Red Bull Bar&Store in Milan

S – STRENGHTS	W – WEAKNESSES
• Well-established Brand names with strong customer loyalty • High acceptance by different market groups like youngsters and sportsmen • Offer unique and new products like a wide range of variations of Red Bull drink	• Lack of experience in running a bar • High establishment cost • Lack of innovation • Reliance on small product variety
O – OPPORTUNITIES	T - THREATS
• Demand for variation of beverages • Expansion of target market • Need for relationship marketing	• Keen competition • Spreaded rumors about the formula of the drink resulted in negative publicity • Legal issue and law regulations • Stagnant market growth in a relatively saturated energy drink market

Project Charter

The next step was to create the Project Charter. It provides us a preliminary description of roles and responsibilities, outlines the project scope and objectives and defines the authority of the project manager.

The image below shows the initial version of our Project Charter.

After some deeper research and precise calculation during our project we had to make some changes regarding the date/period of the main events and the estimated budget. As this has been the first Bar&Store opening for the Red Bull company, we couldn't at the beginning of this project make a clear statement of how high the costs of this project will be and how long each task will take. The Project Charter has been modified and the latest version can be found in the appendix.

PROJECT CHARTER

Group Nr.:	3

Team Member:	Alessandro Pezzoli
Team Member:	Diana Inan
Team Member:	Mauro Tommaso De Candia
Team Member:	Sixtine Le Chatelier
Team Member:	Thea Klein
Team Member:	Weronika Dąbrowska
Team Member:	Fan Yuen Ching

Project Title:	Redbull Bar&Store in Milan		
Project Sponsor:	Red Bull	Date Prepared:	26.02.2013
Project Manager:	Weronika Dąbrowska	Project Customer:	Red Bull customers

Project Purpose or Justification (Scope):

The Red Bull Company wants to undertake a project that would promote its brand with a new message. The main aim of this project is not to increase income, but to strengthen the image of the brand, gain new customers and enter new market. Opening the bar is a part of company's marketing strategy. It wants to show different ways of drinking its principal Red Bull energy drink and in the long term, increase sales of the product. What is more Red Bull Company wants its brand to be associated with sport's events, active style of life and social interactions.

Project Description

Red Bull Company wants to open in Milan the bar, under the company's name "Red Bull". In this bar customers will be able to buy various kinds of Red Bull products, energy cocktails, soft drinks etc. People would be able to sit there, listen to music, watch sports events on the screens and have a good time.
What is more, in the same place, there will be the small Red Bull corner store with variety of Red Bull gadgets, like t-shirts, caps, but also sportswear and accessories.
The place would be open from 10am till 2am, 7 days a week.

Project (and Product) Requirements & Acceptance Criteria:

By selling Red Bull energy drinks and variety of unique cocktails with Red Bull, the company wants to rediscover the image of its brand as a part of marketing strategy. This marketing strategy will effect in an increase of the sales in the future.

The inside of the place should reflect the image that Red Bull wants to spread, which is sporty, fancy, chilling, a place where you go to have an extreme experience.

Moreover, the project is unique for company but also for the whole drink producers industry. Because of this, it has set a great challenge to meet the expectations of the stakeholders.

To accept the results of our projects the stakeholders expect to see the real increase in sales and revenues as a return on their investment. On the other hand this place should meet the expectations of all the Red Bull fans and customers to live the exciting experience the company has promised to them.

Initial Risks:

Unexpected costs
Problems with external companies
Time management
Not meet the expectations of the stakeholder → if the project will not be successful
Losing customers, who would be unsatisfied with the switch of image and disagree with this projects

Summary of Main Events, Phases or Milestones	Date/Period
Creation of a marketing concept: target group analysis, determination of customer needs.	6 weeks 1. CW 1 - 7.CW 6
Site planning (city, area size, contract...)	8 weeks 1. CW 7 - 7. CW 14
suppliers selection and common product development	5 weeks 1.CW 7 - 7. CW 11
bar planning (staff, concept for interior & exterior design, corporate design, realization, planning of bar opening)	10 weeks 1. CW 15 - 7. CW 24
BAR OPENING	End

OPENING A RED BULL BAR&STORE IN MILAN

Estimated Budget:

We estimated that revenues from clothes will be 10% of revenues from drinks. So, we forecast to sell 100,000 drinks and 2,500 clothes in the first year and we hypothesize that the average receipt will be 5€ for drinks and 20€ for clothes. (for didactic reasons we do not consider the VAT)

Sales Budget	Drinks	Clothes	Total
Sales volumes	100,000	2,500	102,500
Average receipt	€ 5	€ 20	
Revenues	€ 500,000	€ 50,000	€ 550,000

Since the idea is to sell Red Bull associated with other types of drinks, creating cocktail based on Red Bull, and sell various types of clothing, for simplicity we decided to take into account the average variable cost per unit of each drink and item of clothing.
We hypothesized to have 4 employees with an annual salary of € 25,000 per year.

Costs Budget	Drinks	Clothes	Total
Sales volumes	100,000	2,500	102,500
Average variable cost per unit	€ 1	€ 5	
Total variable costs	€ 100,000	€ 50,000	€ 150,000
Renting			€ 30,000
Accountant fee			€ 2,000
Scheduled maintenance			€ 2,000
Insurance premium			€ 1,000
Marketing and advertising bar			€ 4,000
Financial expenses			€ 1,000
Salaries			€ 100,000
Total fixed costs			€ 140,000
TOTAL COSTS			**€ 290,000**

We hypothesized that the place in which to open the Red Bull bar was rented.

Investments Budget	Total
Start-up costs	€ 10,000
Furniture	€ 40,000
Equipment	€ 20,000
Total investments	€ 70,000

We decided to depreciate the initial investment of 70,000 euro in ten years, so every year we have a depreciation of 7,000 euro.
We assumed a tax burden of 40%.

Economic Budget	Total
Total revenues	€ 550,000
Total variable costs	- € 150,000
Total fixed costs	- € 140,000
Depreciation	- € 7,000
Profit before taxes	€ 253,000
Taxes (40%)	- € 101,200
Net profit	€ 151,800

According to our estimates, the project generates a profit.

Project Manager Authority Level

The project manager of this project would be responsible for:
- the authority on each phase of the overall project
- planning and organizing the task step by step.
- controlling the effects
- dividing the tasks between team members
- finance side of the project
- reporting the advancement of the project to investors and stakeholders

Approvals: *(Not Required)*

_____ _____
Project Manager Signature   Sponsor or Originator Signature

_____ _____
Project Manager Name   Sponsor or Originator Name

_____ _____
Date   Date

3. WBS & MILESTONES

WBS

The WBS divides a project into the following aspects: Project, phases and activities. It depends on the project if there are 1st level, 2nd or 3rd level activities. At the top of the model is the name of the project. The next level shows the phases and activities in a hierarchy form. The WBS model is important to clarify the project and to reach the general goal of the project by organising secondary goals because it is easier to control. The WBS also represents the foundation for detailed cost estimating and providing guidance for schedule development.

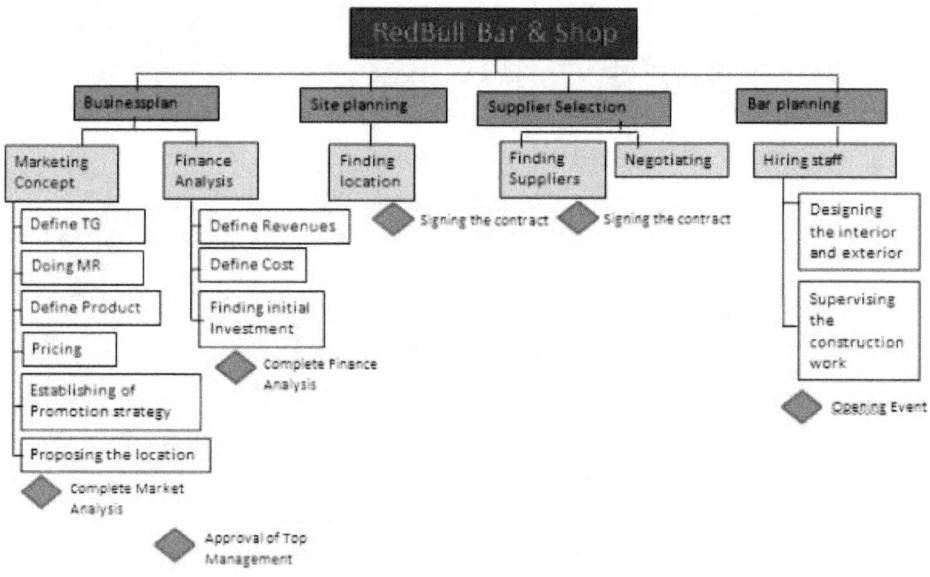

WBS of our project: Opening a Red Bull Bar & Shop

Explanation:

We divided our project in four phases:

1. Business plan, 2. Site planning, 3. Supplier Selection, 4. Bar planning.

The first phase is called Business plan. In order to finish the phase there are a lot of activities to do. The first level activities are divided into doing Marketing Concept and Finance analysis. The Finance Analysis is also separated into three 2nd level activities which have to be done. Concerning the Marketing Concept there are six 2nd level activities which have to be finished. After the market analysis and financial analysis is a milestone to guarantee that these activities are finished. After completing the whole phase there is a Milestone called „Approval of Top Management" because after this phase including research and defining the target group and cost, the top Management needs to approve the project to provide money in order to realize the project. The second phase is site planning there is one 1st level activity which is to find a location. This phase is ended by the Milestone named „signing the contract"and represents an intermediate scope. The third phase is the supplier selection and contained two 1st level activities to find suppliers and negotiate with them. After finishing the activities there is another milestone to have an intermediate in order to control the project of its success. The milestone is the signage of a contract with the supplier. The fourth phase is the Bar planning. The 1st level activity is to hire staff for the shop, because without any staff the 2nd level activities designing and supervising cannot be done. There is another milestone after the last phase to finalize the project and to reach the general goal of the project: the opening event.

Milestones

Milestones are specific results to reach during the project. Generally, there are milestones after each phase which represents intermediate scopes. The project Red Bull Bar& Store consists of four phases and includes six milestones:

1. Complete marketing analysis
2. Complete financial analysis
3. Approval of Top Management
4. Signing the contract
5. Signing the contract
6. Opening Event

The milestones are intermediate scopes which need to be achieved to continue with the project. We decided to set Milestones after the 1st level activities of the first phase to guarantee that the analysis is finished before starting with the implementation. Afterwards, when the whole phase is finished is a milestone called the Approval of the top Management which is required to provide the needed money for the project. Moreover, it is a milestone which also shows if the top Management supports the project and think that it is successful. The second and the third milestones are the signage of contracts with the owner of the location and the supplier which is needed to process the project. The last milestone is the opening event, because if all activities are finished the opening event can go on process and the project will be finished.

4. DESCRIPTION OF TASK ACTIVITIES

There are total 4 phases under the entire project; namely the Business Plan, Site Planning, Suppliers Selection, and Bar Planning. 1st and 2nd levels of activities can be found. The task descriptions are as followings:

Phase1: Business Plan

1.1 Marketing concept

1.1.1 Defining target group:

We have to define who will be our customers, by means of social (demographic) variables like age, gender, lifestyle, income and occupation; as well as geographic variables (how many customers live in our reachable area).

1.1.2 Doing market research:

If we want to open a bar we have to do the market research. We have to analyze the macro environment by analyzing existing competition, substitute products, and preparing SWOT/PEST/5 5 Porters Analysis.

1.1.3 Defining product:

We want to define what products we want to sell in our bar and store. (Packaging, labeling, ingredients, the ways we want to deliver the products to the clients).

1.1.4 Pricing:

After analyzing the competition and target group, we need to define the suitable cost and competitive pricing strategy; in order to be cost - effective and profitable.

1.1.5 Establishing promotion strategy:

We need to think how to promote and advertise our products both inside the bar and in the market by using marketing promotional channels such as materials, gadgets, tasting of products.

1.1.6 Proposing the location:

We analyze shopper traffic in the area so as to find the best location for our bar. We should also get research about the costs of renting the preferred area.
The initial milestone is the completion of marketing analysis.

1.2 Finance analysis

1.2.1 Defining revenues:

We have to define how much money we can get from selling drinks and other products in our bar. We should prepare the estimated sales budgets which will show the yearly amount of income.

1.2.2 Defining cost:

We have to define all the cost that our activity will incur. We have to compare the costs with forecasted revenues to decide if our activity is profitable or what should be carried out to justify the costs.

1.2.3 Finding initial investment:

We have to find the source of capital to open and maintain our bar & store. That means that we have to propose our ideas to Red Bull Company and lobby for the investments.

The following milestone is the completion of financial analysis; while the milestone of the entire Phase 1 is the approval of top Management.

Phase 2: Site planning

2.1 Finding location:

We have to do the on-site investigation to decide the final location for our store, with reference to previous analyses.
The milestone of this phase is the signing of the contract.

Phase 3: Suppliers selection

3.1 Finding suppliers:

To find suppliers we have to do the comparative analysis of what is available on the market. Find the most efficient suppliers for products that we sell in the bar.

3.2 Negotiating with suppliers:

This is the part in which we have to negotiate with suppliers to obtain the best deals and conditions for our partnership.
The milestone of this phase is the signing of the contract.

Phase 4: Bar planning

4.1 Hiring staff

We have to define what kinds of staff we need in our store and bar. Deciding what competencies are required for each position is thus critical. Finally we have to interview the shortlisted candidates and hire the most suitable staff.

4.2 Designing the interior and exterior

We have to choose and hire an external designing company that would be responsible for both the exterior and interior design of the Red Bull bar and store to create a welcoming atmosphere.

4.3 Supervising the construction work

As we have to assign the construction activity to an external company, regular check on the work in progress is needed in

charge by our staff of the project team.
The milestone of this phase is the Opening Event.

5. OBS & RAEW MATRIX

In our Organizational Breakdown Structure is easily shown the hierarchical decomposition according with our WBS' activities. The Project Manager is the highest figure on the OBS as well as the Authority holder over the all phases. Below him we can find the second hierarchical level with the Activities' Directors, each one Responsible over the Work of their respective Teams. All the people belonging to the second level are horizontally interconnected, which means people Responsible for each phase have to take in consideration plans approved and decisions taken in the previous phases under the Authority of the Project Manager. 'Previous phases' because it fits with the Gantt chart as well (phase two apart), so that we can consider it a 'Timeline Connection' between phases, as indicated by the grey timeline.

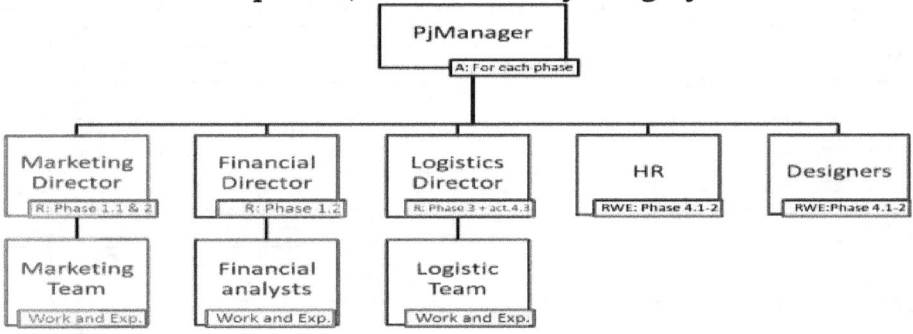

We can notice it more clearly on the REAW Matrix where the colors follow the same order highlighted by the arrow verse on our OBS (->), even if structuring by Activities and not by hierarchy. As shown in the table below the color order Black, Green,

Blue, Orange, Purple is respected as it was horizontally in the OBS (except for phase 2). The hierarchical composition of our OBS helps empowering the Directors over their respective working teams but in the same time enhance intra-communication among them.

Looking at the RAEW Matrix it comes up first of all that Responsibility, Work and Expertise are assigned mostly on hierarchical base. This could mean rigidity in case of 3 or more levels of activities as well as in a complex organization but not in our case where the organizational structure have been maintained simple and each phase is wisely split on a competence basis.

This means no connection between bottom levels, where each Employee is directed by the related Director only, and not even among directors during each phase but just an 'Informational Update' between phases. The Project Manager, holding the Authority on the overall Project, is facilitated by our structure in monitoring and coordinating the all phases, whereas the planning activity of each Director is based on the Project Manager trust on their experience and competencies.

RAM	PjM	Marketing Director	Marketing team	Financial Director	Financial team	Logistics director	Logistics team	HR	Designer
Redbull Bar & Store									
Business Plan									
Marketing concept									
Defining target group	a	r	we						
Doing market research	a	r	we						
Defining product	a	r	we						
Pricing	a	r	we						
Establishing promotion strategy	a	r	we						
Proposing the location	a	r	we						
Complete marketing analysis	a								
Finance analysis									
Defining revenues	a			r	we				
Defining costs	a			r	we				
Finding initial investment	a			r	we				
Complete financial analysis	a								
Approval of top Management	a								
Site planning									
Finding location	a	r	we						
Signing the contract	a								
Supplier selection									
Finding suppliers	a					r	we		
Negotiating with suppliers	a					r	we		
Signing the contract	a								
Bar planning									
Hiring staff	a							rwe	
Designing the interior and exterior	a								rwe
Supervising construction work	a						r	we	
Opening event	a								

6. LOGICAL NET AND GANTT

The Logical Network

The Logical Network visually establishes the sequence of activities in a project. It shows which activity logically precedes or follows another activity, which activities need to be completed in order to start the next one, etc. It gives a graphical overview over the logical sequence of all the work packages that have to be done.

In order to build this logical net, let's go back to the WBS details of our project:

I- Business plan

    1) Marketing concept
        1. Defining Target Group
        2. Doing market research
        3. Defining product
        4. Pricing
        5. Establishing promotion strategy
        6. Proposing the location
    2) Finance analysis
        1. Defining revenues
        2. Defining cost
        3. Finding initial investment

II- Site planning

    1) Finding location

III- Suppliers selection

    1) Finding suppliers
    2) Negotiating with suppliers

IV- Bar planning

    1) Hiring staff
    2) Designing the interior and exterior
    3) Supervising the construction work

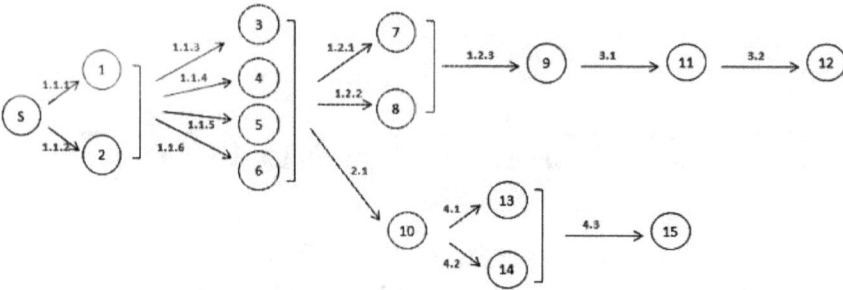

Let's now try to understand how it works and how it is designed:

Obviously, the project starts with the establishment of the business plan, and the first activities of the Marketing Concept, which aim at defining the target customers (1.1.1) and doing all the market research (1.1.2) are two activities that can easily be done at the same time. Then, once all of this preliminary marketing research has been done, we can go on to the next set of activities, which can also be defined as marketing, but on another level. It is the set up of a more applied marketing strategy, regarding the choice of the products to sell (1.1.3), the pricing strategy (1.1.4), the whole promotion strategy (1.1.5) and the first proposal of location possibilities (1.1.6). From this point on, enough elements will have been gathered to start thinking about finance and budgeting, with the targeted revenues and costs (1.2.1 and 1.2.2); but in the same time, we can also start working on a real and deeper location search (2.1), as we should have all the necessary information in mind. Thus, our logical net divides itself into two branches, one mainly focused on the supplier selection, with the research of suppliers (3.1) preceding the negotiation (3.2); and the other branch focusing on the concrete planning of the bar opening, hiring the staff (4.1), then working on the design of the bar (4.2) and finally supervising the work (4.3) in order to open.

The Gantt Chart

The Gantt Chart is a bar diagram that arises directly from the logical net, but adding a time notion to every activities, as well as the milestones. Thus, the succession of the activities is obviously the same as we've seen just above. Let's now focus on the timescale chosen for each activity.

First of all, it is important to consider the notion of "working time", that is not the same as the "elapsed time". Indeed, the timescale used in the Gantt Chart only counts the working days. The total number of days accounted as 120 for our entire project would then account to approximately 24 real time weeks.

Here is an explanation table to comment our choices of time allocation. It is important to realize that the time given is with arbitrary deadlines given to our different working teams. There is no regular time associated to each of these tasks in general, so we fixed the deadlines that seemed the most appropriate considering the work that had to be done for each activity.

1	**Business Plan**		
1.1	**Marketing concept**		
1.1.1	Defining Target Group	10 days	Find information (demo, geo, …) and study it
1.1.2	Doing market research	30 days	Analyzing existing competition, substitute products, preparing SWOT/PEST/5 Porters Analysis
1.1.3	Defining product	10 days	What products to sell
1.1.4	Pricing	10 days	What pricing strategy
1.1.5	Establish promotion strat.	10 days	Develop the marketing mix
1.1.6	Proposing the location	7 days	Analyze shopping traffic by area and renting costs.
	Complete mark. analysis	*0*	*Milestone*
1.2	**Finance analysis**		
1.2.1	Defining revenues	10 days	Draw the sales forecasting plan
1.2.2	Defining cost	10 days	Draw the list of all costs (everyday running)

1.2.3	Finding initial investment	15 days	Research and negotiation with companies, Red Bull etc...
	Complete fin. analysis	*0*	*Milestone*
	Approval of Top Management	*0*	*Milestone*

2	**Site planning**		
2.1	Finding location	30 days	6 weeks seem right to find and negotiate for the "walls" of our bar
	Signing the contract	*0*	*Milestone*

3	**Suppliers selection**		
3.1	Finding suppliers	15 days	Analysis of suppliers available and their value
3.2	Negotiating with suppliers	10 days	Enter in contact and reach an agreement
	Signing the contract	*0*	*Milestone*

4	**Bar planning**		
4.1	Hiring staff	15 days	Time for HR activities to take place
4.2	Designing the int & ext	20 days	4 weeks for working with designers
4.3	Supervising construction	30 days	6 weeks for construction (as there is no hard work to do, just redesign)
	Opening Event	*0*	*Milestone*

OPENING A RED BULL BAR&STORE IN MILAN

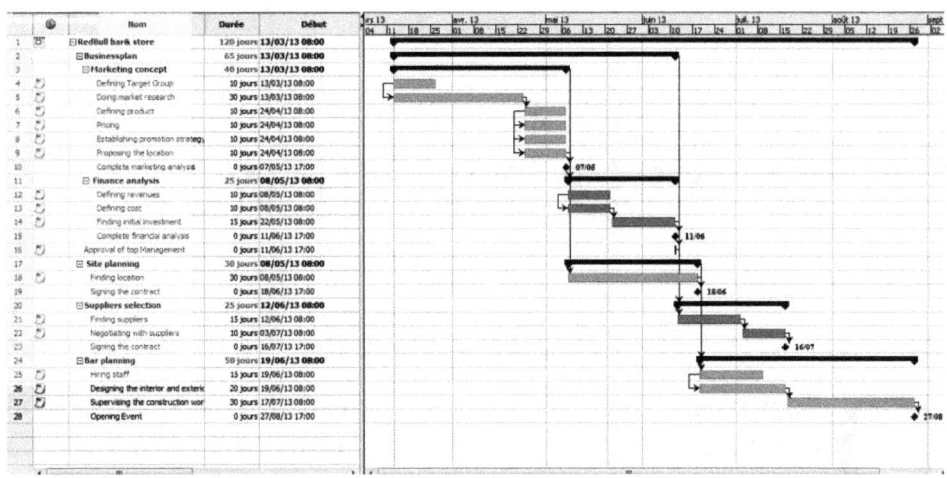

Our GANTT Chart:

7. CBS & COST ANALYSIS

Our project involves the whole preliminary stage of the bar opening that sells drinks and clothes. The main steps to follow before the opening are:
1. The drafting of a business plan that includes marketing activities (such as the definition of the product, the target and market research) and financial analysis (such as the definition of revenues and costs and research of funding)
2. The search for a place where start the business
3. The selection of suppliers
4. The planning of the bar by the research staff designing the interior and exterior of the bar with the installation of furnishings and equipment.

The first three activities generate costs with mainly intellectual work while the last activity absorbs more than half of the costs due to the installation of furnishings and equipment.

The following show a table in which there is a list of professionals involved in our project and as a result their daily and monthly salaries (calculated on a hypothesis month consists of 22 working days). Also you can see how many days every professional has participated in the project and the costs generated by their work.

Payroll	Monthly Wage	Daily Wage	Working Days	Payroll
Project Manager	6.600,00	300,00	120	36.000,00
Marketing Director	4.400,00	200,00	70	14.000,00
Marketing Team (2 people)	2.200,00	100,00	70	7.000,00
CFO	4.400,00	200,00	25	5.000,00
Financial Team (2 people)	2.200,00	100,00	25	2.500,00
Logistic Director	4.400,00	200,00	55	11.000,00
Logistic Team (2 people)	2.200,00	100,00	55	5.500,00
HR	4.400,00	200,00	15	3.000,00
Designer	4.400,00	200,00	20	4.000,00
			Total cost of staff	88.000,00

Once we have established what the costs of staff are, we proceeded to draw up another table in which we have divided the personnel costs on the basis of hours worked for each activity. All this has allowed us to identify what are the activities that have required more financial resources.

Activity/Staff	Project M.	Marketing D.	Marketing T. (2 p.)	CFO	Financial T. (2 p.)	Logistic D.	Logistic T. (2 p.)	HR	Designer	TOTAL
Defining product	250,00	500,00	250,00							1.000,00
Pricing	250,00	500,00	250,00							1.000,00
Establishing promotion strategy	250,00	500,00	250,00							1.000,00
Proposing the location	250,00	500,00	250,00							1.000,00
Product marketing	1.000,00	2.000,00	1.000,00							4.000,00
Defining target group	1.000,00	2.000,00	1.000,00							4.000,00
Doing market research	5.000,00	4.000,00	2.000,00							11.000,00
Marketing concept	7.000,00	8.000,00	4.000,00							19.000,00
Defining revenues	500,00			1.500,00	750,00					2.750,00
Defining costs	500,00			1.500,00	750,00					2.750,00
Finding initial investment	2.000,00			2.000,00	1.000,00					5.000,00
Finance analysis	3.000,00			5.000,00	2.500,00					10.500,00
Business Plan	10.000,00	8.000,00	4.000,00	5.000,00	2.500,00					29.500,00
Finding location	9.000,00	6.000,00	3.000,00							18.000,00
Site planning	9.000,00	6.000,00	3.000,00							18.000,00
Finding suppliers	5.000,00					3.000,00	1.500,00			9.500,00
Negotiating with suppliers	3.000,00					2.000,00	1.000,00			6.000,00
Supplier selection	8.000,00					5.000,00	2.500,00			15.500,00
Hiring staff	2.000,00							3.000,00		5.000,00
Designing the interior and exterior	3.000,00								4.000,00	7.000,00
Supervising construction work	4.000,00					6.000,00	3.000,00			13.000,00
Bar planning	9.000,00					6.000,00	3.000,00	3.000,00	4.000,00	25.000,00
Payroll	36.000,00	14.000,00	7.000,00	5.000,00	2.500,00	11.000,00	5.500,00	3.000,00	4.000,00	88.000,00

After that, we proceeded to identify what could be other types of costs that each activity could incur. In the first three phases we have identified cost of stationery and transport in the case of employees who had to travel to different places to do market research, select suppliers, travel to various banks to find financing, etc.

The following show instead a table in which there is a detailed list of furniture needed for the design of the bar. We have omitted to list the equipment due to too technical complexity.

	Units	Price per unit	TOTAL
Kitchen	1	€ 3.100,00	€ 3.100,00
Cupboard	12	€ 400,00	€ 4.800,00
Sofa	2	€ 2.000,00	€ 4.000,00
Table	12	€ 400,00	€ 4.800,00
Chair	72	€ 75,00	€ 5.400,00
Toilette	6	€ 1.200,00	€ 7.200,00
Lighting	22	€ 250,00	€ 5.500,00
TV	4	€ 1.000,00	€ 4.000,00
Mirror	20	€ 60,00	€ 1.200,00
		Total	€ 40.000,00

OPENING A RED BULL BAR&STORE IN MILAN

Activity/Nature	Start-up costs (work)	Furniture	Equipment, stationery and transport costs	Total	Percentage
Defining product	1.000,00		100,00	1.100,00	0,74%
Pricing	1.000,00		100,00	1.100,00	0,74%
Establishing promotion strategy	1.000,00		100,00	1.100,00	0,74%
Proposing the location	1.000,00		100,00	1.100,00	0,74%
Product marketing	4.000,00		400,00	4.400,00	2,97%
Defining target group	4.000,00		200,00	4.200,00	2,84%
Doing market research	11.000,00		300,00	11.300,00	7,64%
Marketing concept	19.000,00		1.300,00	20.300,00	13,72%
Defining revenues	2.750,00		100,00	2.850,00	1,93%
Defining costs	2.750,00		100,00	2.850,00	1,93%
Finding initial investment	5.000,00		300,00	5.300,00	3,58%
Finance analysis	10.500,00		500,00	11.000,00	7,43%
Business Plan	29.500,00		1.800,00	31.300,00	21,15%
Finding location	18.000,00		600,00	18.600,00	12,57%
Site planning	18.000,00		600,00	18.600,00	12,57%
Finding suppliers	9.500,00		300,00	9.800,00	6,62%
Negotiating with suppliers	6.000,00		100,00	6.100,00	4,12%
Supplier selection	15.500,00		400,00	15.900,00	10,74%
Hiring staff	5.000,00		100,00	5.100,00	3,45%
Designing the interior and exterior	7.000,00		100,00	7.100,00	4,80%
Supervising construction work	13.000,00	40.000,00	17.000,00	70.000,00	47,30%
Bar planning	25.000,00	40.000,00	17.200,00	82.200,00	55,54%
Redbull Bar&Store	88.000,00	40.000,00	20.000,00	148.000,00	100,00%
Percentage	59,46%	27,03%	13,51%	100,00%	

After having analyzed what are the costs and how they should be distributed in the different activities, you can proceed with the establishment of the CBS.

8. APPENDIX:

New version of the Project Charter

PROJECT CHARTER

Group Nr.:

Team Member: Alessandro Pezzoli
Team Member: Diana Inan
Team Member: Mauro Tommaso De Candia
Team Member: Sixtine Le Chatelier
Team Member: Thea Klein
Team Member: Weronika Dąbrowska
Team Member: Fan Yuen Ching

Project Title: Redbull Bar&Store in Milan

Project Sponsor: Red Bull CEO   Date Prepared: 26.02.2013

Project Manager: Weronika Dąbrowska   Project Customer: Red Bull customers

Project Purpose or Justification (Scope):

The Red Bull Company wants to undertake a project that would promote its brand with a new message. The main aim of this project is not to increase income, but to strengthen the image of the brand, gain new customers and enter new market. Opening the bar is a part of company's marketing strategy. It wants to show different ways of drinking its principal Red Bull energy drink and in the long term, increase sales of the product. What is more Red Bull Company wants its brand to be associated with sports events, active style of life and social interactions.

OPENING A RED BULL BAR&STORE IN MILAN

Project Description

Red Bull Company wants to open in Milan the bar, under the company's name "Red Bull". In this bar customers will be able to buy various kinds of Red Bull products, energy cocktails, soft drinks etc. People would be able to sit there, listen to music, watch sports events on the screens and have a good time.
What is more, in the same place, there will be the small Red Bull corner store with variety of Red Bull gadgets, like t-shirts, caps, but also sportswear and accessories.
The place would be open from 10am till 2am, 7 days a week.

PROJECT CHARTER

Project (and Product) Requirements & Acceptance Criteria:

By selling Red Bull energy drinks and variety of unique cocktails with Red Bull, the company wants to rediscover the image of its brand as a part of marketing strategy. This marketing strategy will effect in an increase of the sales in the future.
The inside of the place should reflect the image that Red Bull wants to spread, which is sporty, fancy, chilling, a place where you go to have an extreme experience.
Moreover, the project is unique for company but also for the whole drink producers industry. Because of this, it has set a great challenge to meet the expectations of the stakeholders.
To accept the results of our projects the stakeholders expect to see the real increase in sales and revenues as a return on their investment. On the other hand this place should meet the expectations of all the Red Bull fans and customers to live the exciting experience the company has promised to them.

Initial Risks:

Unexpected costs
Problems with external companies
Time management
Not meet the expectations of the stakeholder → if the project will not be successful
Losing customers, who would be unsatisfied with the switch of image and disagree with this projects

Summary of Main Events, Phases or Milestones	Date/Period
Phase 1: Business Plan • Marketing concept (Defining Target Group, Doing market research, Defining product, Pricing, Establish promotion strategy, Proposing the location) →*Milestone: Complete marketing analysis* • Finance analysis (Defining revenues, Defining cost, Finding initial investment) →*Milestone: Complete financial analysis* →*Milestone: Approval of Top Management*	112 days
Phase 2: Site Planning (Finding location) →Milestone: *Signing the contract*	30 days
Phase 3: Suppliers selection (Finding suppliers, Negotiating with suppliers, Signing the contract) →Milestone: *Signing the contract*	25 days
Phase 4: Bar planning (Hiring staff, Designing the internal & external area, Supervising construction) →*Milestone: Opening Event*	65 days

PROJECT CHARTER

Estimated Budget:

Activity/Nature	Start-up costs (work)	Furniture	Equipment, stationery and transport costs	Total	Percentage
Defining product	1.000,00		100,00	1.100,00	0,74%
Pricing	1.000,00		100,00	1.100,00	0,74%
Establishing promotion strategy	1.000,00		100,00	1.100,00	0,74%
Proposing the location	1.000,00		100,00	1.100,00	0,74%
Product marketing	4.000,00		400,00	4.400,00	2,97%
Defining target group	4.000,00		200,00	4.200,00	2,84%
Doing market research	11.000,00		300,00	11.300,00	7,64%
Marketing concept	**19.000,00**		**1.300,00**	**20.300,00**	**13,72%**
Defining revenues	2.750,00		100,00	2.850,00	1,93%
Defining costs	2.750,00		100,00	2.850,00	1,93%
Finding initial investment	5.000,00		300,00	5.300,00	3,58%
Finance analysis	**10.500,00**		**500,00**	**11.000,00**	**7,43%**
Business Plan	**29.500,00**		**1.800,00**	**31.300,00**	**21,15%**
Finding location	18.000,00		600,00	18.600,00	12,57%
Site planning	**18.000,00**		**600,00**	**18.600,00**	**12,57%**
Finding suppliers	9.500,00		300,00	9.800,00	6,62%
Negotiating with suppliers	6.000,00		100,00	6.100,00	4,12%
Supplier selection	**15.500,00**		**400,00**	**15.900,00**	**10,74%**
Hiring staff	5.000,00		100,00	5.100,00	3,45%
Designing the interior and exterior	7.000,00		100,00	7.100,00	4,80%
Supervising construction work	13.000,00	40.000,00	17.000,00	70.000,00	47,30%
Bar planning	**25.000,00**	**40.000,00**	**17.200,00**	**82.200,00**	**55,54%**
Redbull Bar & Stone	**88.000,00**	**40.000,00**	**20.000,00**	**148.000,00**	**100,00%**
Percentage	**59,46%**	**27,03%**	**13,51%**	**100,00%**	

PROJECT CHARTER

Project Manager Authority Level

The project manager of this project would be responsible for:

- the authority on each phase of the overall project
- planning and organizing the task step by step.
- controlling the effects
- dividing the tasks between team members
- finance side of the project
- reporting the advancement of the project to investors and stakeholders

Approvals: *(Not Required)*

_____   _____
Project Manager Signature   Sponsor or Originator Signature

_____   _____
Project Manager Name   Sponsor or Originator Name

_____   _____
Date   Date

www.ingramcontent.com/pod-product-compliance
Lightning Source LLC
Chambersburg PA
CBHW050325220526
45465CB00005B/2139